THE INVESTIGATOR

Delving Into Enneagram 5

Asa Eccleston Kibilski

CONTENTS

THE INVESTIGATOR UNVEILED: AN INTRODUCTION TO ENNEAGRAM TYPE 5

In the intricate tapestry of human personalities, the Enneagram offers a unique lens through which to understand ourselves and others. Each of the nine Enneagram types represents a distinct worldview, a set of core motivations, and a unique path to growth and fulfillment. In this chapter, we delve into the enigmatic world of Enneagram Type 5, often called "The Investigator."

The Investigator is a thinker, an observer, a seeker of knowledge and understanding. They are driven by a deep-seated need to comprehend the world around them, to gather information, and to make sense of the complexities of life. This thirst for knowledge is not simply a matter of intellectual curiosity; it is a fundamental aspect of their being, a way of navigating and coping with the world.

At their core, Investigators are motivated by a fear of being incompetent or incapable. This fear drives them to amass knowledge and skills, to become experts in their chosen fields, and to avoid situations where they might feel exposed or overwhelmed. They value independence and self-sufficiency, preferring to rely on their own resources and expertise rather than seeking help from others.

This desire for independence can sometimes lead Investigators to withdraw from the world, to seek solitude and quiet contemplation. They may feel overwhelmed by the demands of social interaction and prefer to spend their time immersed in books, research, or other solitary pursuits. However, it is important to note that this withdrawal is not necessarily a sign of misanthropy or aversion to people; rather, it is a reflection of their need for space and time to recharge their mental and emotional batteries.

Investigators are often drawn to intellectual pursuits, such as science, philosophy, or the arts. They are attracted to fields that offer opportunities for in-depth research, analysis, and problem-solving. They are natural observers, able to see patterns and connections that others might miss. They are also often gifted with a sharp wit and a dry sense of humor, which they may use to deflect attention from their own vulnerabilities.

While the Investigator's thirst for knowledge and independence are undoubtedly strengths, they can also become challenges. The constant pursuit of information can lead to information overload and a feeling of being overwhelmed. The desire for self-sufficiency can isolate them from others and make it difficult to form close relationships. The fear of being incompetent can lead to perfectionism and a reluctance to take risks.

Despite these challenges, Investigators are capable of great depth and insight. They are often gifted with a unique perspective on the world, a way of seeing things that others might miss. They are loyal friends, insightful mentors, and valuable contributors to their communities. By understanding their strengths, challenges, and motivations, Investigators can learn to embrace their unique gifts and live more fulfilling lives.

THE THINKING CENTER: HOW TYPE 5S NAVIGATE THE WORLD THROUGH THOUGHT

In the intricate landscape of the Enneagram, each personality type is associated with a primary center of intelligence: the Head (Thinking), the Heart (Feeling), or the Gut (Instinct). For Type 5s, the Investigators, the Head Center reigns supreme. This is where they process information, make decisions, and interact with the world. Understanding this dominant center is key to unraveling the intricacies of the Type 5 personality.

The Thinking Center is the realm of intellect, analysis, and observation. Type 5s, as quintessential thinkers, are naturally drawn to this realm. They are driven by a thirst for knowledge, a desire to understand the underlying principles and patterns that govern the world around them. This thirst is not merely an intellectual exercise; it's a core aspect of their identity, a way of making sense of their experiences and finding a sense of security in a complex and often chaotic world.

For Investigators, thinking is not just a mental activity; it's a way of life. They observe the world with a keen eye, constantly analyzing and interpreting the information they gather. They are drawn to complex ideas and systems, seeking to understand the intricate workings of everything from scientific phenomena to human behavior. This intellectual curiosity is often accompanied by a deep skepticism, a reluctance to accept information at face value without thorough examination and analysis.

This reliance on the Thinking Center can be both a strength and a challenge. On one hand, it allows Type 5s to develop a deep understanding of the world around them. They are often able to see patterns and connections that others might miss, and they can use this insight to solve complex problems and make sound decisions. However, this reliance on thinking can also lead to overthinking, analysis paralysis, and a tendency to get lost in their own thoughts.

Type 5s may also struggle with emotional expression and connection, as their focus on thinking can lead to a disconnect from their own feelings and the feelings of others. They may view emotions as messy, unpredictable, and potentially overwhelming, preferring to maintain a distance from them. This can make it difficult to form close relationships and to navigate the emotional complexities of life.

Despite these challenges, the Thinking Center is a powerful tool for Type 5s. By understanding its strengths and limitations, they can learn to harness its power for personal growth and fulfillment. They can develop strategies for managing their tendency to overthink, for connecting with their emotions, and for building meaningful relationships with others. They can also use their intellectual gifts to make valuable contributions to their communities and to the world at large.

In the chapters ahead, we will explore the core motivations and fears that drive Type 5s, the different ways in which they manifest their Thinking Center dominance, and the paths they can take to achieve greater balance and integration. By delving deeper into the world of the Investigator, we can gain a richer understanding of this fascinating and complex Enneagram type.

CORE MOTIVATIONS AND FEARS: THE DRIVING FORCES BEHIND THE INVESTIGATOR

At the heart of every Enneagram type lies a complex interplay of core motivations and fears. These deep-seated drivers shape our behaviors, our perceptions, and our interactions with the world around us. For Type 5s, the Investigators, these motivations and fears are deeply intertwined, creating a unique dynamic that fuels their quest for knowledge and understanding.

The primary motivation for Type 5s is the pursuit of knowledge and understanding. They are driven by an insatiable curiosity, a thirst to comprehend the world in all its complexity. This thirst is not merely an intellectual exercise; it's a fundamental need, a way of navigating the world and finding a sense of security in its often chaotic nature. For Investigators, knowledge is power, a way to gain mastery over their environment and to protect themselves from the unknown.

This pursuit of knowledge is often accompanied by a desire for independence and self-sufficiency. Type 5s value their autonomy and prefer to rely on their own resources and expertise rather than seeking help from others. This stems from a fear of being incompetent or incapable, a fear that drives them to become experts in their chosen fields and to avoid situations where they might feel exposed or overwhelmed. They seek to create a safe and secure environment for themselves, one where they can control their surroundings and avoid being dependent on others.

This desire for independence can sometimes manifest as a tendency to withdraw from the world, to seek solitude and quiet contemplation. Type 5s may feel overwhelmed by the demands of social interaction and prefer to spend their time immersed in books, research, or other solitary pursuits. This withdrawal is not necessarily a sign of misanthropy or aversion to people; rather, it's a reflection of their need for space and time to recharge their mental and emotional batteries.

The fear of being incompetent or incapable is a powerful motivator for Type 5s. It drives them to amass knowledge and skills, to become experts in their chosen fields, and to avoid situations where they might feel exposed or vulnerable. This fear can also lead to perfectionism, a reluctance to take risks, and a tendency to procrastinate or avoid tasks that they feel unprepared for.

However, this fear can also be a source of strength. It can fuel a relentless pursuit of knowledge, a determination to overcome obstacles, and a commitment to excellence. By facing their fears and embracing their vulnerabilities, Type 5s can tap into their inner resilience and achieve great things.

Understanding the core motivations and fears of Type 5s is essential for navigating their complex inner world. By recognizing the driving forces behind their behaviors, we can gain a deeper appreciation for their unique strengths and challenges. We can also develop strategies for supporting their growth and development, for helping them overcome their fears, and for fostering a deeper sense of connection and belonging.

THE 5 WITH A 4 WING: THE CREATIVE INVESTIGATOR (THE ICONOCLAST)

In the intricate world of the Enneagram, the concept of "wings" adds another layer of complexity and nuance to each type. A wing is the adjacent Enneagram type that influences the core type, subtly shaping its characteristics and behaviors. For Type 5s, the Investigators, the 4 wing (The Individualist) brings a unique blend of creativity, emotional depth, and intensity to their analytical minds.

The 5 with a 4 wing, often called the "Creative Investigator" or "Iconoclast," embodies a fascinating paradox. They are both deeply intellectual and profoundly emotional, driven by a thirst for knowledge yet also attuned to the nuances of their inner world. This combination of head and heart creates a unique perspective, a way of seeing the world that is both analytical and imaginative.

The influence of the 4 wing can manifest in several ways. Creative Investigators may be drawn to artistic or creative pursuits, using their analytical minds to explore complex themes and express their emotions through various mediums. They may also have a deep appreciation for beauty and aesthetics, seeking out experiences that resonate with their soul. This aesthetic sensibility can extend to their personal lives, as they may be drawn to unconventional or unique forms of self-expression.

The 4 wing can also intensify the Type 5's tendency towards introspection and self-reflection. Creative Investigators may spend significant time exploring their inner world, delving into their emotions, and seeking to understand their unique identity.

This introspection can lead to a deep sense of self-awareness and a rich inner life, but it can also lead to feelings of isolation and alienation if not balanced with healthy social connections.

In relationships, the 5 with a 4 wing may be both intensely passionate and fiercely independent. They crave deep, meaningful connections but also need ample space and solitude to recharge their emotional batteries. They may struggle with vulnerability and self-disclosure, preferring to maintain a certain level of emotional distance. However, when they do open up, their depth of feeling and insight can be profoundly moving.

The Creative Investigator's path to growth involves finding a balance between their intellectual and emotional sides. They can benefit from exploring their creativity, expressing their emotions through art or other outlets, and cultivating meaningful relationships with others. They can also learn to embrace their unique individuality and to find joy and fulfillment in their own unique way of being in the world.

The 5 with a 4 wing is a complex and multifaceted personality type, full of contradictions and paradoxes. They are both deeply intellectual and profoundly emotional, both fiercely independent and intensely passionate. By understanding and embracing their unique blend of traits, they can unlock their full potential and live a life that is both meaningful and fulfilling.

THE 5 WITH A 6 WING: THE LOYAL INVESTIGATOR (THE PROBLEM-SOLVER)

The Enneagram's system of wings offers a fascinating exploration of the subtle variations within each type. For the Type 5 Investigator, the 6 wing (The Loyalist) introduces a unique blend of practicality, loyalty, and community-oriented thinking to their analytical nature. This combination gives rise to the 5 with a 6 wing, often called the "Loyal Investigator" or "Problem-Solver."

Unlike the 5 with a 4 wing, who leans towards introspection and emotional depth, the 5 with a 6 wing is more outwardly focused and pragmatic. They channel their intellectual curiosity towards practical solutions and tangible outcomes. This grounded approach often leads them to fields where they can utilize their knowledge and skills to address real-world problems and contribute to the greater good.

The 6 wing's influence is evident in the Loyal Investigator's strong sense of duty and responsibility. They are deeply committed to their communities, organizations, and chosen causes. This loyalty can manifest in various ways, from volunteering their time and expertise to advocating for social justice issues. They are often drawn to roles where they can use their analytical skills to support and protect others, such as law enforcement, social work, or community organizing.

This sense of loyalty also extends to their personal relationships. The 5 with a 6 wing values trust and commitment, seeking to build lasting connections with people they can rely on. They may be more open and approachable than other Type 5s, willing to share their knowledge and insights with those they trust. This willingness to collaborate and share can be a valuable asset in both personal and professional settings.

However, the 6 wing's influence can also bring its own set of challenges. The Loyal Investigator's sense of duty and responsibility can sometimes lead to overthinking and anxiety. They may worry about making the wrong decision or letting others down, leading to analysis paralysis or avoidance of risk-taking. Their loyalty to others can also lead them to neglect their own needs and boundaries, potentially leading to burnout or resentment.

The path to growth for the 5 with a 6 wing involves finding a balance between their need for security and their desire to contribute to the world. They can benefit from cultivating self-compassion, learning to trust their own instincts, and setting healthy boundaries in their relationships. They can also explore ways to channel their intellectual curiosity and problem-solving skills towards projects that align with their values and passions.

The 5 with a 6 wing is a unique and valuable personality type, offering a blend of intellectual rigor and community-oriented thinking. They are loyal friends, dedicated problem-solvers, and passionate advocates for the causes they believe in. By understanding and embracing their unique strengths and challenges, they can make a significant contribution to the world while also finding personal fulfillment and happiness.

INVESTIGATOR STRENGTHS: INQUISITIVE MINDS AND DEEP FOCUS

The Enneagram Type 5, the Investigator, possesses a unique set of strengths that allow them to navigate the world with remarkable insight and depth. These strengths are not merely surface-level traits but are deeply rooted in their core motivations and cognitive processes. Understanding these strengths is key to appreciating the unique contributions that Investigators make to their personal lives, their professions, and society as a whole.

One of the most prominent strengths of the Investigator is their insatiable curiosity and thirst for knowledge. They possess an innate drive to understand the world around them, to delve deep into complex subjects, and to uncover hidden patterns and connections. This intellectual curiosity is not merely a passing interest; it is a fundamental aspect of their being, a driving force that fuels their personal and professional pursuits.

This thirst for knowledge is often accompanied by a remarkable capacity for deep focus and concentration. Investigators can spend hours immersed in research, analysis, or problem-solving, their minds fully engaged in the task at hand. This ability to concentrate allows them to achieve a level of mastery and expertise in their chosen fields that is often unparalleled. They are not easily distracted or deterred, and they possess a remarkable capacity for sustained effort and attention to detail.

Investigators are also gifted with a keen eye for observation and analysis. They are able to see patterns and connections that others might miss, and they can synthesize vast amounts of information into coherent and insightful conclusions. This analytical ability is not limited to academic or intellectual pursuits; it can be applied to a wide range of situations, from understanding complex social dynamics to solving practical problems in the workplace.

Another strength of the Investigator is their independence and self-sufficiency. They are not afraid to go against the grain, to challenge conventional wisdom, and to forge their own path. This independent spirit can be a source of great creativity and innovation, as they are not bound by the constraints of traditional thinking. They are also able to work autonomously, requiring minimal supervision and direction.

The Investigator's strengths are not without their challenges. Their intense focus can sometimes lead to isolation and a neglect of personal relationships. Their independent nature can make it difficult to collaborate with others or to accept help when needed. Their analytical mind can sometimes lead to overthinking and a tendency to get lost in details.

However, by understanding and harnessing their strengths, Investigators can make significant contributions to the world. Their intellectual curiosity, deep focus, and analytical abilities can lead to groundbreaking discoveries, innovative solutions, and profound insights. Their independence and self-sufficiency can inspire others to think for themselves and to challenge the status quo.

In the chapters ahead, we will explore the various ways in which Investigators can leverage their strengths to achieve personal and professional success. We will also discuss the challenges they may face and offer strategies for overcoming them. By embracing their unique gifts and navigating their potential pitfalls, Investigators can live a life that is both meaningful and fulfilling.

INVESTIGATOR CHALLENGES: DETACHMENT, ISOLATION, AND AVERSION TO VULNERABILITY

While Enneagram Type 5s, the Investigators, possess remarkable strengths, they are not without their challenges. These challenges are often deeply ingrained in their personality structure and can manifest in various ways, impacting their relationships, emotional well-being, and overall life satisfaction. Understanding these challenges is a crucial step towards personal growth and self-improvement for Investigators.

One of the most common challenges faced by Type 5s is their tendency towards detachment and emotional distance. They may prioritize intellectual pursuits over emotional connection, viewing feelings as messy, unpredictable, and potentially overwhelming. This emotional detachment can create a sense of isolation, making it difficult to form deep and meaningful relationships with others. It can also lead to a lack of self-awareness and an inability to recognize or express their own emotions.

This emotional distance can be a defense mechanism, a way to protect themselves from feeling overwhelmed or vulnerable. Investigators may fear that opening up to others will expose their weaknesses or make them dependent on others. They may also feel that their emotions are not as valid or important as their intellectual pursuits. However, this emotional suppression can have negative consequences, leading to a sense of emptiness, loneliness, and dissatisfaction.

Another challenge faced by Investigators is their aversion to vulnerability. They may feel that showing their emotions or asking for help is a sign of weakness or incompetence. This can lead to a reluctance to seek support from others, even when it is needed. It can also create a sense of isolation and prevent them from forming close relationships.

The Investigator's tendency towards isolation can be exacerbated by their need for solitude and quiet contemplation. While this need for alone time is essential for their well-being, it can become a problem if it leads to a complete withdrawal from social interaction. This can lead to feelings of loneliness, depression, and a lack of connection with others.

These challenges are not insurmountable. By understanding their tendencies towards detachment, isolation, and aversion to vulnerability, Investigators can take steps to overcome them. They can learn to identify and express their emotions, to build healthy relationships, and to seek support when needed. They can also cultivate a greater sense of self-compassion and acceptance, recognizing that their emotions are valid and important.

The path to growth for Type 5s involves embracing their emotional side and finding a balance between their intellectual and emotional needs. By doing so, they can unlock a deeper level of self-awareness, connection with others, and overall life satisfaction. They can also discover that vulnerability is not a weakness but a source of strength, allowing them to form deeper and more meaningful relationships with others.

RELATIONSHIPS AND THE INVESTIGATOR: NAVIGATING CONNECTIONS WITH OTHERS

The realm of relationships presents a unique landscape for Enneagram Type 5s, the Investigators. Their introspective nature, preference for solitude, and tendency towards emotional detachment can pose challenges in forming and maintaining deep connections with others. Yet, beneath their reserved exterior lies a yearning for genuine connection, a desire to share their insights and knowledge with those they trust. This chapter delves into the intricate dance of relationships for the Investigator, exploring their strengths, challenges, and pathways to deeper connection.

Investigators approach relationships with a cautious yet discerning eye. They value quality over quantity, preferring a few close, meaningful connections to a wide circle of acquaintances. They seek out individuals who share their intellectual curiosity, who can engage in stimulating conversations, and who respect their need for space and autonomy. For them, trust and mutual understanding are paramount, and they may take time to open up and reveal their true selves to others.

One of the challenges Investigators face in relationships is their tendency towards emotional distance. They may struggle to express their feelings openly and may find it difficult to empathize with the emotions of others. This can create a sense of disconnect in relationships, leaving their partners feeling unfulfilled or misunderstood. However, with conscious effort and a willingness to step outside their comfort zone, Investigators can learn to access and express their emotions, fostering deeper intimacy and connection.

Another challenge is their need for solitude and independence. While this need is essential for their well-being, it can sometimes be misinterpreted as aloofness or disinterest by their partners. This can lead to misunderstandings and conflicts, especially if their partners have different needs for connection and intimacy. Open communication and a willingness to compromise are crucial for navigating these differences and creating a harmonious relationship.

Despite these challenges, Investigators bring unique strengths to their relationships. Their intellectual curiosity and insightful nature can make them fascinating conversationalists and thoughtful partners. They are often loyal and supportive, offering a listening ear and practical advice when needed. Their analytical minds can also be helpful in problem-solving and navigating challenges together.

Investigators can thrive in relationships where their need for independence and intellectual stimulation is respected. Partners who value their unique perspective and appreciate their depth of knowledge can create a fulfilling and supportive partnership. By cultivating open communication, emotional vulnerability, and a willingness to step outside their comfort zone, Investigators can build lasting and meaningful connections with others.

Ultimately, relationships for the Investigator are a journey of self-discovery and growth. By embracing their strengths and challenges, they can cultivate deeper connections, experience greater intimacy, and find true fulfillment in their relationships. It is a journey that requires patience, understanding, and a willingness to embrace vulnerability, but the rewards are immeasurable.

GROWTH PATHS FOR TYPE 5S: EMBRACING FEELING, ACTION, AND CONNECTION

While the Investigator's analytical mind and thirst for knowledge are undeniable strengths, their journey towards personal growth often involves venturing beyond their comfort zones. Enneagram Type 5s can unlock a wealth of untapped potential by embracing the realms of feeling, action, and connection, areas that may not come as naturally to them but are essential for a balanced and fulfilling life.

The realm of feeling, often neglected by the Investigator, is a rich and nuanced landscape waiting to be explored. By allowing themselves to feel and express their emotions, Type 5s can connect with a deeper level of authenticity and vulnerability. This can lead to greater self-awareness, stronger relationships, and a more vibrant sense of aliveness. While it may feel uncomfortable or even overwhelming at first, learning to embrace their emotional landscape can be a transformative experience.

One way for Type 5s to access their emotions is through creative expression. Engaging in activities such as writing, painting, music, or dance can provide a safe and expressive outlet for their feelings. These creative endeavors can also help them tap into their intuition and imagination, enriching their intellectual pursuits with a touch of emotional depth.

In addition to feeling, the Investigator's growth journey involves stepping into the realm of action. While they may be adept at analyzing and planning, they can sometimes get stuck in their heads, overthinking and delaying action. By cultivating a willingness to take risks, to experiment, and to learn from their mistakes, Type 5s can break free from the paralysis of analysis and turn their ideas into reality. This can be as simple as starting a new hobby, volunteering for a cause they care about, or taking on a new challenge at work.

The realm of connection is another area where Type 5s can expand their horizons. Their preference for solitude and independence can sometimes lead to isolation and a lack of meaningful relationships. By consciously seeking out social interaction, engaging in activities with others, and cultivating deeper connections with friends and family, Investigators can discover the joy and fulfillment that comes from sharing their lives with others. This may involve stepping outside their comfort zone and initiating conversations, joining social groups, or simply spending more time with loved ones.

Embracing feeling, action, and connection is not about abandoning the Investigator's intellectual strengths but rather about integrating them with other aspects of their being. By cultivating a more holistic approach to life, Type 5s can achieve greater balance, resilience, and well-being. This journey of growth is not always easy, but it is a worthwhile endeavor that can lead to a more fulfilling and meaningful life.

As Type 5s embark on this journey, it is important to remember that growth is a process, not a destination. It is about taking small steps, experimenting with new approaches, and celebrating the victories along the way. By embracing their vulnerability, stepping into the unknown, and connecting with others on a deeper level, Investigators can unlock their full potential and live a life that is both rich in knowledge and abundant in love and connection.

THE INVESTIGATOR AT WORK: IDEAL CAREERS AND WORKPLACE DYNAMICS

The Enneagram Type 5, the Investigator, brings a unique set of skills and perspectives to the workplace. Their thirst for knowledge, analytical minds, and ability to focus deeply make them valuable assets in a variety of professions. However, their preferences for autonomy, intellectual stimulation, and clear boundaries can also shape their ideal work environments and interactions with colleagues.

Investigators thrive in careers that allow them to utilize their intellectual curiosity and problem-solving skills. They are often drawn to fields that require in-depth research, analysis, and critical thinking. This can include careers in science, technology, engineering, mathematics, academia, or any field that allows them to explore complex ideas and systems. They are also well-suited for roles that require independent work and minimal supervision, as they value autonomy and the freedom to pursue their interests.

In the workplace, Investigators tend to be reserved and focused, preferring to work independently or in small teams. They may not be the most outgoing or social colleagues, but they are often respected for their expertise and insights. They are reliable, detail-oriented, and committed to producing high-quality work. However, their tendency to overthink and their aversion to conflict can sometimes create challenges in team settings.

Investigators value clarity and structure in the workplace. They prefer well-defined roles and responsibilities, clear expectations, and open communication. They may struggle in environments that are chaotic, ambiguous, or overly emotional. They also need ample time and space for independent work, as they recharge their batteries through solitude and reflection.

When collaborating with others, Investigators can be valuable team members. They bring a unique perspective, a wealth of knowledge, and a keen eye for detail. However, they may need to be encouraged to share their ideas and insights, as they may not always be comfortable speaking up in group settings. They also need to be mindful of their tendency to become overly critical or dismissive of others' ideas.

To create a positive and productive work environment for Investigators, it is important to recognize and respect their unique needs. This includes providing them with opportunities for intellectual stimulation, allowing them autonomy and independence in their work, and creating a clear and structured work environment. It is also important to foster open communication and encourage them to share their ideas and insights.

By understanding the Investigator's strengths and challenges in the workplace, both employers and colleagues can create a more harmonious and productive work environment. This can lead to greater job satisfaction, increased productivity, and a more positive workplace culture for everyone involved.

STRESS AND THE INVESTIGATOR: RECOGNIZING AND MANAGING TYPE 5 STRESS PATTERNS

In the intricate dance of life, stress is an inevitable partner, a force that tests our resilience and challenges our well-being. For Enneagram Type 5s, the Investigators, stress can trigger a unique set of responses, often rooted in their core motivations and fears. Understanding these stress patterns is crucial for navigating life's challenges and maintaining emotional and mental equilibrium.

Under stress, Investigators tend to withdraw further into their inner world, seeking refuge in their thoughts and analyses. They may isolate themselves from others, seeking solitude and quiet contemplation. This withdrawal can be a coping mechanism, a way to regain a sense of control and understanding in the face of overwhelming circumstances. However, if left unchecked, it can lead to further isolation, emotional detachment, and a deepening of their core fears.

Another common stress response for Type 5s is an intensification of their analytical tendencies. They may overthink, obsess over details, and become consumed by their thoughts. This can lead to a feeling of being overwhelmed and a sense of losing touch with reality. They may also become more critical and judgmental of themselves and others, leading to strained relationships and a sense of alienation.

As stress levels rise, Investigators may become increasingly avoidant and scattered. They may procrastinate on tasks, neglect their responsibilities, and find it difficult to focus or make decisions. They may also become more sensitive to criticism and feedback, feeling easily overwhelmed or threatened by perceived attacks.

These stress responses are not merely individual quirks; they are deeply rooted in the Investigator's core fears of incompetence, vulnerability, and being overwhelmed. When faced with stress, these fears can become amplified, leading to a cascade of negative emotions and behaviors.

Fortunately, there are strategies that Investigators can employ to manage their stress and avoid falling into unhealthy patterns. One approach is to cultivate mindfulness and self-awareness. By paying attention to their thoughts, emotions, and bodily sensations, they can recognize the early signs of stress and take steps to address them before they escalate.

Another strategy is to engage in activities that promote relaxation and well-being. This could include exercise, spending time in nature, practicing meditation or yoga, or engaging in creative pursuits. By prioritizing self-care and finding healthy outlets for their stress, Investigators can maintain their emotional and mental balance.

It is also important for Type 5s to build a strong support network of trusted friends, family, or professionals. These individuals can offer a listening ear, a different perspective, and encouragement during challenging times. By reaching out for help and support, Investigators can avoid isolation and find the strength to overcome their stressors.

Ultimately, managing stress for Type 5s is about finding a balance between their need for solitude and their need for connection, between their intellectual pursuits and their emotional well-being. By cultivating self-awareness, engaging in self-care, and building strong relationships, Investigators can navigate life's challenges with greater resilience and grace.

THE INVESTIGATOR'S SPIRITUAL JOURNEY: SEEKING MEANING AND TRANSCENDENCE

In the depths of the Investigator's intellectual pursuits often lies a yearning for something more, a quest for meaning and transcendence that goes beyond the confines of the material world. This spiritual journey is a unique and often solitary path, marked by introspection, contemplation, and a thirst for deeper understanding.

For Type 5s, spirituality is not always about organized religion or traditional beliefs. It can be a deeply personal and individualistic exploration, a search for truth and meaning that transcends the limitations of the human mind. This quest can take many forms, from studying philosophy and metaphysics to exploring mystical traditions and contemplative practices.

At the heart of the Investigator's spiritual journey is a desire to understand the interconnectedness of all things. They seek to uncover the underlying patterns and principles that govern the universe, to see beyond the surface of reality and grasp the deeper truths that lie beneath. This quest for understanding can be a source of great inspiration and awe, as they glimpse the vastness and complexity of existence.

For some Investigators, spirituality is a way to connect with a higher power or a sense of universal consciousness. This connection can provide a sense of comfort, guidance, and belonging, filling the void that their independent nature sometimes creates. It can also offer a sense of purpose and meaning, helping them to see their place in the grand scheme of things.

Others may find spiritual fulfillment in the pursuit of knowledge and wisdom. They may see their intellectual pursuits as a way to expand their consciousness and connect with the deeper truths of existence. This can lead to a profound sense of fulfillment and a feeling of being part of something larger than themselves.

The Investigator's spiritual journey is often marked by periods of solitude and introspection. They may spend time meditating, journaling, or simply contemplating the mysteries of life. This solitary reflection allows them to connect with their inner wisdom and to gain insights that are not always accessible through intellectual analysis.

However, the Investigator's journey is not always a solitary one. They may seek out spiritual communities or teachers who can offer guidance and support. They may also find solace in connecting with nature, art, or music, which can offer glimpses of the transcendent and inspire a sense of awe and wonder.

The Investigator's spiritual journey is a lifelong process of exploration and discovery. It is a journey that can lead to greater self-awareness, a deeper sense of meaning and purpose, and a profound connection with the universe. By embracing their spiritual nature, Investigators can tap into a source of wisdom and guidance that can enrich their lives and help them navigate the complexities of the human experience.

INTEGRATING THE INVESTIGATOR: PRACTICAL TOOLS FOR PERSONAL GROWTH

The journey of personal growth for the Enneagram Type 5, the Investigator, is a fascinating exploration of self-discovery and integration. It involves embracing their strengths, addressing their challenges, and finding a balance between their intellectual pursuits and their emotional well-being. This chapter delves into practical tools and strategies that Investigators can utilize to navigate this journey, fostering greater self-awareness, resilience, and fulfillment.

One of the most powerful tools for personal growth is self-reflection. By taking the time to observe their thoughts, emotions, and behaviors, Investigators can gain valuable insights into their inner workings. Journaling, meditation, or simply spending quiet time in contemplation can help them connect with their deeper selves and identify patterns that may be holding them back. This self-awareness is the first step towards making positive changes and embracing their full potential.

Another valuable tool is mindfulness. By paying attention to the present moment without judgment, Investigators can cultivate a greater sense of awareness and acceptance. This can help them manage stress, regulate their emotions, and connect more deeply with themselves and others. Mindfulness practices such as meditation, yoga, or simply taking a few minutes each day to focus on their breath can be transformative for Type 5s.

Therapy or counseling can also be a valuable resource for Investigators seeking to deepen their self-understanding and overcome challenges. A skilled therapist can provide a safe and supportive space for them to explore their emotions, identify their core beliefs, and develop strategies for personal growth. Therapy can also help them address any underlying issues that may be contributing to their detachment, isolation, or aversion to vulnerability.

In addition to these individual practices, Investigators can also benefit from engaging in activities that promote emotional expression and connection with others. This could include joining a support group, taking a creative class, or simply spending more time with loved ones. By stepping outside their comfort zone and engaging with the world in new ways, they can expand their horizons and discover new sources of joy and fulfillment.

Another key aspect of personal growth for Type 5s is developing healthy coping mechanisms for stress and anxiety. This could involve learning relaxation techniques, such as deep breathing or progressive muscle relaxation, or engaging in activities that promote physical and emotional well-being, such as exercise or spending time in nature.

The journey of integrating the Investigator is a lifelong process, one that requires patience, self-compassion, and a willingness to embrace change. It is about finding a balance between their intellectual pursuits and their emotional needs, between their desire for solitude and their need for connection. By utilizing practical tools and strategies, Investigators can embark on a transformative journey of self-discovery, leading to greater self-awareness, resilience, and overall well-being.

SELF-CARE FOR THE INVESTIGATOR: NOURISHING MIND, BODY, AND SPIRIT

In the relentless pursuit of knowledge and understanding, the Investigator, the Enneagram Type 5, can often neglect their own well-being. Their intense focus and dedication to intellectual pursuits can lead to an imbalance, where the needs of the mind overshadow the needs of the body and spirit. Yet, for true fulfillment and sustained growth, it is essential for Type 5s to prioritize self-care, to nourish all aspects of their being.

Self-care for the Investigator begins with honoring their need for solitude and intellectual stimulation. This means carving out dedicated time for reading, research, or simply quiet contemplation. It means creating a space where they can retreat from the demands of the external world and recharge their mental batteries. Whether it's a cozy reading nook, a well-stocked library, or a peaceful corner of nature, finding a sanctuary for solitude is essential for the Investigator's well-being.

However, self-care goes beyond intellectual pursuits. It also involves caring for the body and spirit. Regular exercise, a healthy diet, and sufficient sleep are essential for maintaining physical and mental energy. Engaging in activities that bring joy and relaxation, such as spending time in nature, listening to music, or practicing mindfulness, can also nourish the soul and promote overall well-being.

For the Investigator, self-care can also involve challenging their comfort zones and stepping outside their usual routines. This might mean trying a new hobby, taking a class, or exploring a different genre of literature. By expanding their horizons and engaging in novel experiences, they can stimulate their minds and prevent stagnation.

Self-care can also involve cultivating a sense of emotional awareness and expression. This might involve journaling, talking to a trusted friend or therapist, or engaging in creative activities that allow for emotional release. By acknowledging and expressing their emotions, Investigators can foster a deeper connection with themselves and others, leading to greater emotional well-being and fulfillment.

It is important to note that self-care is not selfish or indulgent. It is a necessary part of maintaining a healthy and balanced life. For Investigators, who are often driven by a strong sense of duty and responsibility, it can be challenging to prioritize their own needs. However, by recognizing that self-care is an investment in their own well-being, they can create a more sustainable and fulfilling life path.

Ultimately, self-care for the Investigator is about finding a harmonious balance between their intellectual pursuits, their physical needs, and their emotional well-being. It is about creating a life that nourishes all aspects of their being, allowing them to thrive both personally and professionally. By prioritizing self-care, they can unlock their full potential and live a life that is both rich in knowledge and abundant in joy and fulfillment.

EMBRACING YOUR INNER INVESTIGATOR: FINDING BALANCE AND FULFILLMENT

The journey of the Investigator, the Enneagram Type 5, is a lifelong exploration of knowledge, understanding, and self-discovery. It is a path marked by intellectual curiosity, a thirst for knowledge, and a desire to make sense of the world's complexities. Yet, it is also a journey of integration, of balancing the mind's insatiable hunger with the needs of the heart and body. This final chapter invites you to embrace your inner Investigator, to celebrate your unique gifts, and to discover the path to true balance and fulfillment.

Embrace your thirst for knowledge, your analytical mind, and your ability to delve deep into the mysteries of life. These are your superpowers, your tools for navigating the world and making meaningful contributions. Celebrate your independence, your self-sufficiency, and your unique perspective on the world. These qualities make you a valuable asset to your communities and a source of inspiration to others.

However, remember that true fulfillment comes from embracing all aspects of your being, not just your intellect. Allow yourself to feel, to experience the full range of human emotions, and to connect with others on a deeper level. Explore your creativity, your passions, and your spiritual nature. These are all vital parts of who you are, and they deserve to be nurtured and expressed.

Find a balance between your need for solitude and your need for connection. Embrace your time alone for reflection and recharge, but also make time for meaningful interactions with others. Cultivate relationships that nourish your soul, that challenge you to grow, and that bring joy and laughter into your life.

Remember that your journey is unique. There is no one-size-fits-all approach to personal growth and fulfillment. Embrace your individuality, your quirks, and your passions. Trust your instincts, follow your curiosity, and never stop learning.

As you embrace your inner Investigator, you may find that your life takes on a new dimension of richness and meaning. You may discover hidden talents, forge deeper connections, and find joy in unexpected places. You may also encounter challenges and setbacks, but with resilience and self-compassion, you can overcome them and emerge stronger.

The path of the Investigator is not always easy, but it is a rewarding one. By embracing your strengths, addressing your challenges, and cultivating a balanced and holistic approach to life, you can unlock your full potential and create a life that is both meaningful and fulfilling. Remember, you are not just an Investigator; you are a complex and multifaceted individual with a unique set of gifts and talents. Embrace your whole self, and let your light shine brightly.